Sss For ?

by Jacqueline Sweeney

photography by G. K. & Vikki Hart
photo illustration by Blind Mice Studio

Evans Brothers Limited

*With thanks to
Judith Puddick, literacy consultant, for writing
the literacy skills activities*

First published in Britain in 2000 by
Evans Brothers Limited
2A Portman Mansions
Chiltern Street
London W1M 1LE

First published by
Benchmark Books
Marshall Cavendish Corporation
99 White Plains Road
Tarrytown, New York 10591

Text copyright © 2000 by Jacqueline Sweeney
Photo illustrations copyright © 2000 by G. K. & Vikki Hart
and Mark & Kendra Empey

British Library Cataloguing in Publication Data
Sweeney, Jacqueline.
Sss For ? – (We can read!)
1. Snakes – Physiology – Juvenile fiction 2. Readers (Elementary)
3. Children's stories
I. Title
428.6

ISBN 0 237 52175 X

Printed in Italy

Characters

Molly

Gus

Tim

Jim

Ron

Ladybird

Hildy

Eddie

Hester

"Look!" squeaked Molly.
"Over there — on Pond Rock!"

"I see it!" yelled Tim.

"It's white," grunted Gus.

"It's flapping," croaked Ron.

"Let's get closer," said Ladybird.

"I'll race you!" quacked Hildy.

Everyone started to run.

9

"It's huge!" cried Ladybird.

"It's small," said Hildy.

"It's smooth," said Molly, "and soft."

"Feels like paper," said Ron.

"Like plastic," said Tim.

Jim squinted. "Is it a cloud?"

"I see tiny stars!" said Gus.

"Diamonds," said Ladybird.

Hildy sang:

Paper and plastic

all in one.

Shines like diamonds

in the sun.

No one heard
the snake's slow slide.
But *everyone* heard
HISS-*S*-*S*-S.

"Eek!" shrieked Molly.
"Help!" squealed Tim.

"S-s-s-s-stop!" hissed Hester.

"Run!" cried Jim.
He ran right into her!

Molly fainted.

Gus hid in his shell.

"Don't be scared," said the snake.

"I'm Grandma Hester."

Her tongue flicked.

"And that's my skin."

"Come back!"

Slowly they moved closer.

"I shed my skin

FOUR times a year," said Hester.

"Why?" asked Ladybird.

Hester smiled.

"So I can grow," she said.

"Like when I lose my feathers?"
asked Hildy.
"When tadpoles lose their tails?"
asked Ron.

"Yes," said Hester.

"Aren't you too old to grow?"
asked Tim.

"Never too old," said Hester.
"I expect I'll grow
all my life."

The sun was low.

"Time to go," said Hester.

PLOP!

She slipped into the pond.

"Will you be *our* Grandma?" called Gus.

"Oh yes-s-s-s," said Hester.

"Will you visit me again?"

"Oh yes,"
said the friends.
"Yes-s-s-s!"

USING 'WE CAN READ' TO DEVELOP LITERACY SKILLS

The following activities based on **Sss For ?** *are designed to support the National Literacy Strategy teaching objectives for Reception and Year 1 children (ages 4 to 6).*

The activities encourage children to:
- *develop their vocabulary*
- *become aware of the relationship between sounds and letters*
- *use their reading to support their writing*
- *make links with other subject areas*

TEXT LEVEL SKILLS

- Ask the children to identify the animals on the cover. What might they be looking at? Talk about the different types of animals. What is the natural habitat for each of them? Which animals might be kept as pets? Can the children predict what the story might be about?

- Take turns to talk about the pictures on each page. Read the text together several times, listening out for the name Hester. Were the children surprised Hester was a grandma snake?

- Talk about grandparents and the different generations in families. Did the children know that snakes shed their skins so often? Can they think why we don't shed our skins? Ask them to re-tell the story in their own words. Talk about the ending. Make up a story together about Hester's return visit, write it out and illustrate the story to make a complete book.

SENTENCE LEVEL

- Look at question sentences in the story and practise reading them with correct intonation. Talk about question marks and tell the children these are special sorts of full stops. Play a guessing game. Find 'Is it a cloud?' in the story and ask the children to use this as a model to write *Is it a ...?* on their own strip of card. Hide an object under a cloth, ask the children to guess what it is and write their guess on their sentence strip, followed by a question mark. They can make as many guesses as they wish but have to write each one down as a question sentence.

- Draw each character and make a speech bubble for each one. Choose one sentence that each character said and write it in the appropriate bubble.

30

WORD LEVEL SKILLS

- **High frequency words:** write *said, it, yes* on separate pieces of card. Give the children one word at a time to find in the book and read the sentences containing these words. Discover which of these words occurs most often. Talk about the 'tricky bit' in *said - ai* making the 'e' sound. Spell the words orally - firstly saying the word, then saying the name of each letter in order, finally saying the word again. Spread out some plastic or wooden letters. Say one of the words and ask a child to write the word by choosing, then arranging the appropriate letters. All say the word, say the letter names in order then say the complete word again. *(Don't encourage children to say the letter sounds when they are learning high frequency words, because so many of these words are irregular.)*

- **Initial and final sounds (phonemes):** Ask the children to draw a snake and practise saying 'sssss'. Listen to some of Hester's hissing words - *HISS-S-S, yes-s-s-s*. Notice the hiss in her name also. Read the story aloud and ask the children to hold up their snakes whenever they hear the 's' sound at the beginning (middle or end) of a word. Write the 's' words on separate pieces of card and ask the children to sort according to the position of 's'. Help the children to write the letter 's' concentrating on the correct formation. Collect pictures and objects containing the 's' phoneme and sort them according to where the 's' sound occurs.

- Try the same activities with the digraph 'sh', asking the children to put one finger over their lips to make the 'sh' sign whenever they hear the sound. Join plastic or wooden letters together with Plasticine or Blu-tac to form 'sh'. Make the other common digraphs 'th', 'ch' and 'ng' also. *(It is important that children see and understand 'sh' to be a digraph i.e. two letters making one sound so they don't try to 'sound out' 's' and 'h' separately.)*

RHYMING COUPLETS

Write out   The sun was low,
                  Time to go.

And help the children to hear the rhyming words.

Try   The sun was high
                  Time to ...

Suggest several more e.g. *The sun was red, time for ...; The sun was bright, time to ....* Think of others for the children to try.

ANIMAL SKINS AND ANIMAL COATS

• Collect together items such as leather, wool, feathers, hair, tortoiseshell, a crab's shell, a snake skin and talk about their textures. Explore contrasting words such as *hard/soft; heavy/light; rough/smooth; warm/cool* and discuss why different animals have such different outside coverings. Encourage the children to choose two favourite words and learn to spell them. Use books to find out more about animal skins, coats and shells.

• Play 'What am I?' Tell the children to write about one of the animals in the story using texture words but without mentioning the animal's name. e.g. 'I have soft fur and a long pink tail. What am I?' Make a 'What am I?' book.

ABOUT THE AUTHOR

Jacqueline Sweeney has published children's poems and stories in many anthologies and magazines, and written numerous professional books on teaching writing.

ABOUT THE PHOTO ILLUSTRATIONS

The photo illustrations are the collaborative effort of photographers G. K. and Vikki Hart and Blind Mice Studio. Following a sketched story board, each animal and element were first photographed individually. The images were then scanned and manipulated. Each illustration may contain from 15 to 30 individual photographs.

All the animals that appear in this book were handled with love. The ladybirds and butterflies were set free in the garden, while the others have been returned to or adopted by loving homes.